WELLINGTON SQUARE

Life during World War Two

Sue Graves

Contents

Why World War Two began

In 1933, Adolf Hitler became the leader of Germany. He wanted Germany to become a very powerful nation. He wanted lots of countries in Europe to become part of a powerful Germany.

First, Adolf Hitler sent his army into Austria.

Then he sent his army into Czechoslovakia.

Time line:

1933		1938	
Hitler becomes leader of Germany		Hitler sends army into Austria	Hitler sends army into Czechoslovaki

In 1939, Adolf Hitler wanted to invade Poland. Britain said that if Hitler invaded Poland then Britain would go to war with Germany.

On 1st September 1939, Adolf Hitler sent his army to invade Poland.

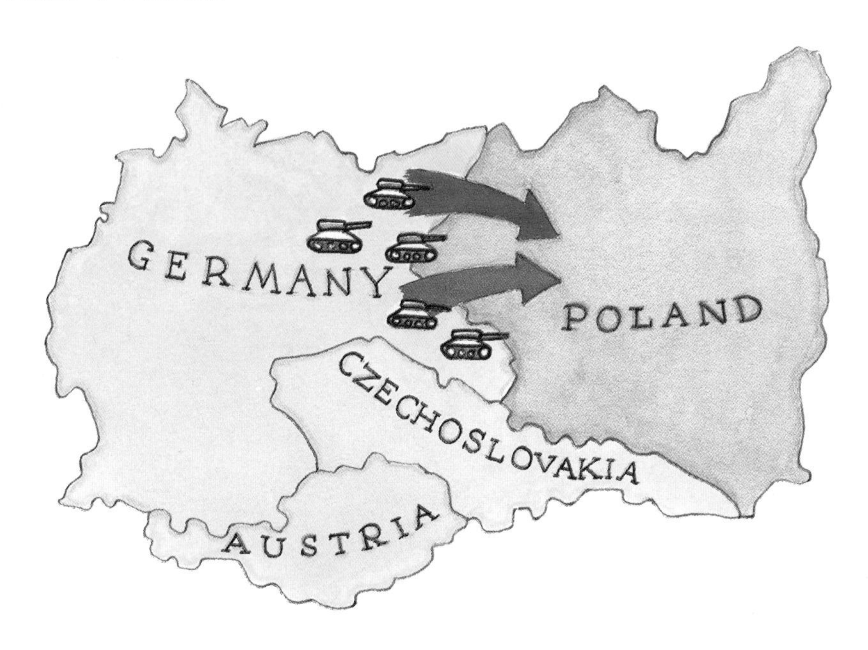

On 3rd September 1939, Britain went to war with Germany.

1939	
Hitler invades Poland	Britain goes to war with Germany

Getting ready for war

People in Britain began to get ready for war. Everyone had to make sure that no lights could be seen at night. The houses had to be blacked out. If lights could be seen from houses, German planes would know where to drop bombs.

Some people put up thick curtains over the windows to hide the lights in their houses.

Some people put black blinds over the windows.

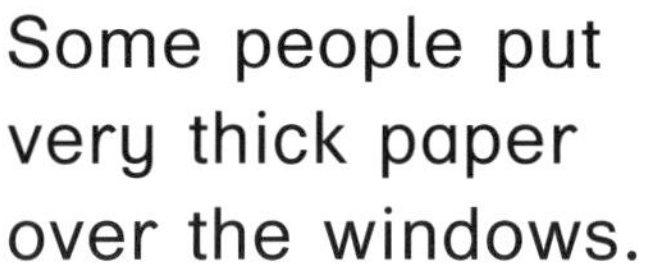

Some people put
very thick paper
over the windows.

Some people painted
their windows with
black paint.

Air-raid wardens
made sure that
no lights were
showing from the
houses.

Shelters

Loud air-raid sirens warned people when air raids were starting. An air raid meant that German planes, carrying bombs, were coming.

The air-raid siren was called 'Moaning Minnie'. It was called 'Moaning Minnie' because of the moaning sound it made.

An air-raid siren

Anderson Shelters

People went to shelters to keep safe from the bombs. Some people had an Anderson Shelter in their garden.

An Anderson Shelter

Morrison Shelters

Some people put up shelters in their homes because they had no gardens. These shelters were called Morrison Shelters. If a house was bombed, the Morrison Shelter would shelter people from falling bricks.

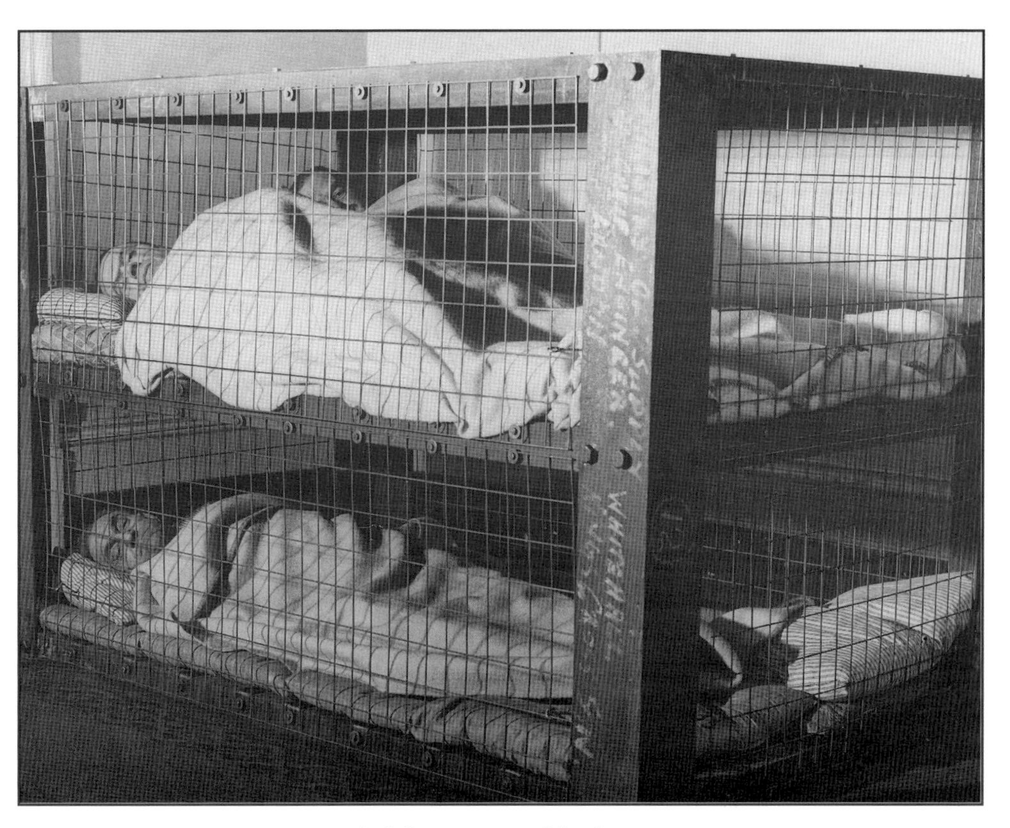

A Morrison Shelter

Other shelters

People sheltered from bombs in lots of other places too.

This family had to shelter in their cellar.

Some people had to shelter in the cupboard under the stairs.

Some people even had to shelter under the kitchen table!

In London, lots of people had to shelter in the underground railway stations. Some people slept on the railway tracks.

People sleeping in the underground railway stations

People could only come out from the shelters when the 'all clear' siren sounded. When they heard this, it meant that the German planes had gone and it was safe to come out.

Food

Before the war, a lot of food was imported into Britain. The food was imported by ships. When World War Two started, many of these ships were sunk by German submarines. Food became very scarce.

Ships bringing food to Britain were sunk by German submarines

Rationing

Foods needed to be rationed. This meant that it had to be shared out so that everyone could have some. In World War Two, everyone was given the same amount of rationed food. Children under five years old were given extra rations.

Ration book

Everyone had a ration book like this. There were coupons inside for milk, eggs, bread, sugar and other foods.

A coupon was torn out of the book when a rationed food was bought.

Children waiting to buy their rations of sweets and chocolates

Rationed foods

All these foods were rationed during the war.

For example, each week you could only have one egg, three pints of dried milk and three eggs' worth of dried egg powder.

Sweets and chocolate were rationed later on in the war, as sugar became scarce.

Eat your vegetables!

Vegetables were not rationed. People were told to eat lots of potatoes, carrots and other vegetables.

People grew vegetables in their gardens instead of flowers.

Some people kept hens so that they could have fresh eggs.

Any leftover scraps of food were put into bins and fed to farm animals.

Evacuees

Many towns were bombed during World War Two. It was not safe for children to live in some of the towns because of the bombs. Many children were sent to live in the countryside where it was safer. These children were called evacuees.

Children being met by billeting officers

The billeting officers had to find foster parents for each child.

Each child had to wear a label on his or her coat. The label had the child's name, school and where they were going, written on it.

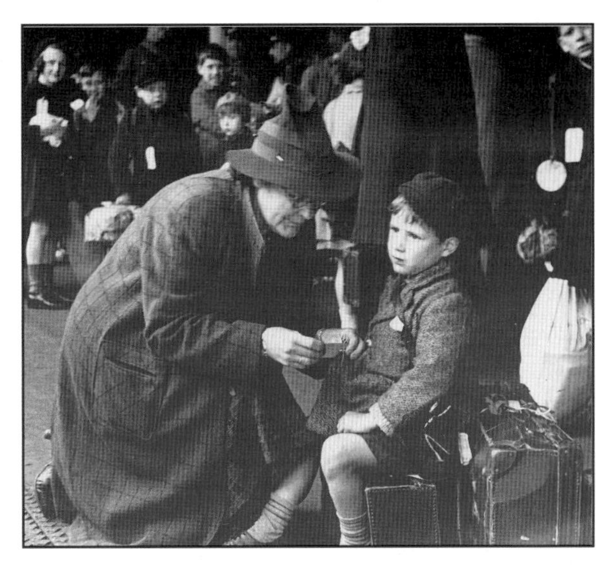

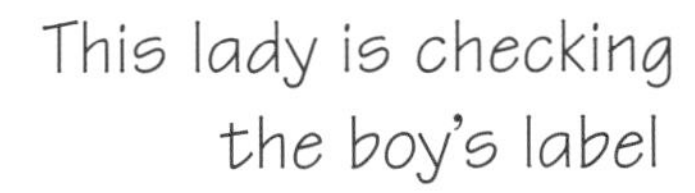

This lady is checking the boy's label

All the children also had to have gas masks with them. The gas mask was kept in a box and worn over the shoulder. Everyone had to have a gas mask in case German planes dropped gas bombs.

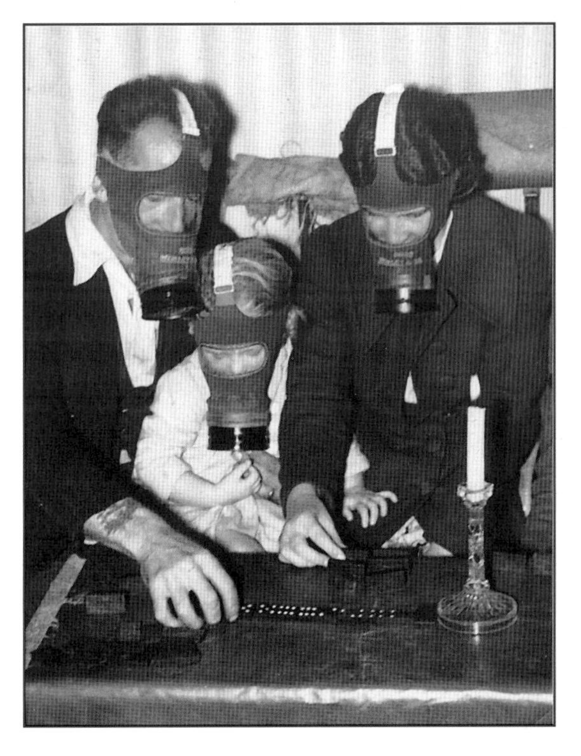

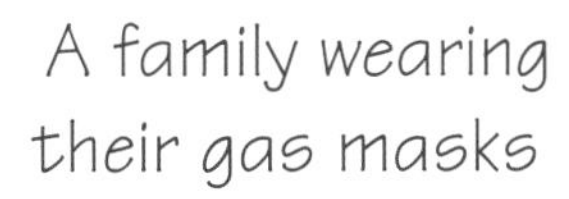

A family wearing their gas masks

Going to school

Going to school was very hard during World War Two. In big towns and cities, some schools were bombed and children had nowhere to go.

This city school was bombed

It was hard to go to school in the countryside, too. So many evacuees came from the towns that they couldn't all fit into the small village schools. Some children had to take it in turns to go to school because there was not enough room for everyone.

There were not as many teachers in schools during World War Two. Male teachers went off to the war to fight as soldiers.

The teachers left in schools were women and older men.

Hitler and the Jewish people

Hitler was a powerful bully. He hated many groups of people such as Jews and gypsies. When he came to power, he told his soldiers to take these people from their home.

Millions of Jewish people were sent to concentration camps. Over six million Jewish people died in concentration camps.

Time line:

1938		193
In April 1938 Hitler sends army into Austria	In March 1939, Hitler sends army into Czechoslovakia	In Septem and Brita

Anne Frank

Anne Frank

Anne Frank was a young Jewish girl who lived in Holland during the war.

She, and her family, hid from the German soldiers. They hid for a long time. Anne wrote a diary about her life in hiding.

Someone told the German soldiers where the family was hiding. Anne and her family were put into a concentration camp where they all died.

After the war, Anne Frank's diary was published.

	1940
9, Hitler invades Poland, to war with Germany	In April, May and June, Hitler invades Denmark, Norway, Holland and Belgium

The end of the war

World War Two with Germany ended in May 1945.
Everyone in Britain was glad that the war was over at long last.

People danced and sang.

Time line:

1941		1945
Hitler invades Russia	USA enters the war	In May, Germany surrenders

Lights and bonfires!

Lights were turned on in the towns for the first time in many years.

There were bonfires and fireworks.

There were big street parties, too.

Glossary

billeting officers – people who found billets or lodgings for evacuees during the war

cellar – a room, underground, for storing things

coupon – a token or ticket

evacuee – a person taken from a dangerous place to a safe place during war

foster parents – people who look after children in place of their parents

imported – goods brought into a country from abroad

invade – to go into another country to take it over

nation – people who live in the same country, speak the same language and have the same government

scarce – when something is scarce it means that you only have a very little of it

shelter – a place where you can hide to keep safe

siren – a signal used to warn people of danger